Work From Home, And Stay Sane!

By

Michael Kaltenbrunner

Michael Kaltenbrunner

Table of Contents

INTRODUCTION 5

Why Do You Want To Work From Home? .6

Reasons Why Working From Home Is Great 7

No More Commuting To Work 7

It's More Comfortable 8

Set Your Own Rhythm.............................9

You Can Be More Productive 10

Who Likes Open-Plan Offices Anyway? .11

Reasons Why Working From Home Is Terrible..12

A Range of New Distractions 12

Eating Too Much Junk 14

Say Goodbye To Your Work Social Life ..15

Should You Work From HOME? 16

Tips To Help You Work From Home And Stay Sane...18

Work And Home Life Balance..................19

Keep You Work Life And Personal Life Separate 19

Sometimes You Must Embrace Distractions...20

Keep Your Family Busy............................20

Make A Door Sign 21

Talk To Your Family 22

Tell Friends To Stay Away 22

Keep Weekends And After Hours Sacred 23

Divide Up Your Work Day 24

Your Workspace 25

Find a Special Work Space......................25

Invest In Making Your Office Space Nice 26

Consider Ergonomics 28

Coffee Shops 30

Should You Rent Some Office Space? 30

Staying Productive 33

It Only Takes Three Seconds To Get Distracted 33

Get Dressed Each Day 34

Don't Sleep All Day 34

Wear Many Hats 35

Make A To-Do Lists And Stick To Them ..35

Be Careful With Your Time Management 36

Eat Lunch At Your Desk 37

Watch Your Snacking 37

The Social Media Trap 38

Unplug The Landline, Internet, Doorbell, Etc. 38

Keeping Yourself Motivated 39

Take Frequent Breaks 40

There Is Always Something Productive To Do 40

FINANCES 42

Get An Accountant 42

Create A Financial Buffer 43

Claim On Work Expenses 43

Taking Care Of You 45

Stay Healthy 45

Make the Most of It...............................46

Get Some Sun and Fresh Air 46

Join a Social Group 47

Make Time for Yourself 47

It Will Get Better...................................48

CONCLUSION 50

INTRODUCTION

Working from home seems like the ultimate dream, right? It's time to kick back and say goodbye to traffic jams, stuffy work shirts, and regular grooming. Well, that's how most people seem to view it: as some sort of utopia where the days are spent relaxing, and maybe the occasional bit of work gets done. If you have this idyllic image of what it will be like to work from home, it might be time for a sobering reality check. Work is still *work*; if nothing gets done, money does not come in, and the bills will quickly start to pile up.

Whether you have already started working at home, or you are thinking about it — this is the ultimate guide to help you do things right. Getting things done is important, but staying sane and keeping your family happy are equally vital.

Why Do You Want To Work From Home?

Deciding whether or not you should work at home is a big deal. It certainly isn't something to be taken lightly, especially if you will need to quit your regular job to do so. Consider the *real* reasons that you think a home job would suit you. As you will learn in following chapters, it's not all fun and games. Most people probably are not cut out for the lifestyle shift that comes with the territory. Take some time to go through the pros and cons, and see if you can have a trial period before you commit to working from your own home.

Reasons Why Working From Home Is Great

No More Commuting To Work

Ah, the daily work commute. What would life be like without that? It would be a lot less stressful, that's for sure. The US Census Bureau listed the average daily commute of US citizens as 25.5 minutes, in 2011. Getting up early and racing to be ready on time is only the start of a day's work, unfortunately. Before you can actually get to the office and give your day away, there is some traveling to be done. Whether you navigate your way through seemingly endless traffic lights and bustling streets, or you cram into the subway with other disgruntled passengers — the daily work commute is not a pleasant thing for anyone.

Working out of the home completely eliminates that commute. Not only can you get out of bed later, but you don't need to worry about even leaving your home. If you like, that extra time can be spent getting more done and earning more money, or even sleeping some more.

It's More Comfortable

Home offices tend to be a lot more comfortable than any other work place. You are not stuck at a desk all day. You can stand up and walk around while you think, or take a phone call. If you feel like stretching and yawning, no one is going to say that you're slacking off. Heck, you can even put your feet up on the desk while you use the computer, because you are at *home*. Do you feel like working on the couch for a bit today? Go ahead, provided that you have a laptop or something to do that doesn't require a desk.

Being comfortable isn't just about having a good seat. More and more of the world's population are sitting for large blocks of time. Many people are glued to their chairs for entire work days, minus a few relatively short breaks. It's not healthy, and research clearly shows that sitting for six or more hours each day greatly increases your chances of dying earlier. Even if you workout regularly, all of that sitting is doing you damage. When you work at home, you can get up and move around as often as you like, provided you are still being productive.

Set Your Own Rhythm

Office hours tend to be between around 9:00am and 5:00pm. Who decided that everyone should work at this time? Some people like to get up extra early, and get things done by midday. Others prefer to sleep in for longer, and work until later at night. Why should everyone in the world have to follow a specific routine, when it only suits certain people?

When you work from home, even if you are still telecommuting with a "regular" employer, it's easier to set your own pace. Do you want to get out of bed at 4:00am and be done for the day by the time most people are having their morning break? Go ahead. Would you like to do some extra work after dinner, so that you can take the following afternoon off to go shopping? That's your choice to make.

However you work best, setting your own rhythm is just one of the perks that comes with working from home.

You Can Be More Productive

Ironically enough, it can be a bit hard to get much done in an office environment. But they are meant to be the most productive places around, right? With all of the meetings that take place, co-workers having conversations and asking questions, and the general interruptions that occur — it's a wonder that anyone can actually get anything done. Even if you are dedicated to staying on task, it can become difficult to shut out noise, overheard chatter and the cacophony of sounds.

Building workplace friendships is great, and office culture can be a rewarding thing, but many workers find they can be a lot more productive when they're in a more isolated environment.

Who Likes Open-Plan Offices Anyway?

A majority of office employees work in open offices. These are essentially just big areas with sectioned off cubicles, where everyone is sharing the same space. Typically, people don't like working in open-plan offices, and it is easy to understand why. The extra stress and lack of privacy that comes with being around so many people, while trying to stay focused, is enough to drive you up the wall. As mentioned in the previous point, people who work at home tend to be more productive, provided that they don't get distracted, but that will be covered in the following pages.

Reasons Why Working From Home Is Terrible

There are a lot of great things about working from home, but it would be silly to assume that it didn't come with just as many bad aspects. Just ask someone who has ever worked out of their house, and they will probably tell you at least a few reasons why it's bad.

A Range of New Distractions

Without a busy office full of people talking

and making noise, it should be easy to stay productive. Well, that *should* be how it goes at least ...

If you will be the only person in your home throughout the day, your chances of getting work done are greatly improved. For anyone who has family members there with them, say hello to new distractions. When people realize that you are home all day, they tend to assume that you are available to talk, or help them do something that is not work related. After all, you can just catch up on work later, right? Maybe you can, but it's easy to get stressed out as tasks build up, if you are not dealing with them during the day.

Family members are not the only distraction at home. There's the issue of having all of your favorite leisure activities right in front of you. There's the TV with all the day time shows that you have been missing. Most likely, you are working on a computer with the Internet — so you have the biggest modern distraction since the television was invented, and no one to make sure that you don't spend half your time watching humorous videos on YouTube, or endlessly scrolling through your Facebook feed.

Even the tiniest distraction can tear you out of "the zone", and leave you spending the next 20 minutes trying to get back on task. Overall, you might spend more hours trying to work, while getting no extra money for the time spend. This can quickly lead to stress and dissatisfaction.

Eating Too Much Junk

Spending every day right near your kitchen can be a bad thing. It does cut down on costs for lunches, and you can have a hot meal if you like. However, the temptation to constantly snack, or order takeout, is ever present. Some people start to stack on the pounds after they shift to working at home, due to less movement, and the easy availability of snacks.

Say Goodbye To Your Work Social Life

Often, good co-workers are the highlight of a person's day. Even when you don't get along with everyone at the office, at least you have the choice of talking to *someone.* It's surprising how much people take those small interactions for granted, because they are just a part of being human. If you decide to work from home, say goodbye to that, unless you share a home office with another person.

For people who thrive on regular socialization, working from home is a bad idea. Do you need to speak with others, and be surrounded by people? If so, it's probably time to accept that you won't be happy at home by yourself.

Should You Work From HOME?

Now that you have looked at some of the best, and worse, things about working from home, take a minute to go over the following list. You should then have a good idea whether you're making the right decision.

Are you …

- A self-starter who gets things done, even with no one to monitor you?
- Able to ignore most distractions, no matter who or what they are?
- Tired of your daily commute?
- Sick of noisy work environments?
- Able to go for entire days without speaking to a single person?
- Organized and highly productive?
- Willing to put in extra work, even when it doesn't immediately result in more money up front?

Did you answer yes to most of these questions? If so, the work from home lifestyle might be perfect for you! If not, maybe your current job isn't so bad after all.

Tips To Help You Work From Home And Stay Sane

Now that you've decided working from home is the best lifestyle for you, it's time to learn how to do so. Anyone can just set up a desk and declare themselves open for business, but that is not going to guarantee those dollars start rolling in. At this point, it's assumed that you are *able* to make money from home somehow. That's not what this book's about. Rather, the following information will help you improve your productivity, happiness, and overall satisfaction with a working from home lifestyle.

Work And Home Life Balance

Keep You Work Life And Personal Life Separate

That building where you live is now going to be both your workplace as well as your home. This is going to cause some problems, at least at first. It's nothing that you cannot learn to deal with. From the very beginning, remember that work time is for working, and all other time is for the rest of your life. Don't start to blur that delicate line that keeps these two unique facets of your life from mixing together.

This is probably one of the most important points in this book, so remember it!

Sometimes You Must Embrace Distractions

There will be times when you cannot avoid being distracted, even if you try. If you're sure that there's no way to get anything done, you might as well enjoy being distracted. So, your kid is home from school for the day, and the baby sitter quit? You might not be able to get any work done at all. Instead of struggling to work, ignoring your restless child, and still managing to do nothing positive — just concede to the fact that you aren't going to work today, and enjoy spending some times with your child.

Keep Your Family Busy

You're not always going to have the house to yourself, even if your kids go to school, and your partner works full time. Does your spouse have a day off work? That's wonderful, but try to make sure that they have something to do — something that does *not* involve your time. Do you need to look after your son or daughter, because they're home sick from school? Make sure they're well taken care of, but try to find a movie for them to watch.

Bored family members who want your time during work hours, are the ultimate enemy to productivity and a steady income stream. There is no need to be abrupt or rude about the matter. Just quietly ensure they have something else to do, or at least help make them more self-sufficient.

Make A Door Sign

It's hard for your family to know if it's okay for them to disturb you, especially if you don't keep regular hours. Try getting a generic shop sign, with "Open" on one side and "Closed" on the other. Hang it outside your office door, and use it to clearly indicate whether or not you are available to talk.

Talk To Your Family

Is this your first time working from home? Don't expect your family members to automatically know how they should act while you're busy. Create a clear signal, so that people know when you are not to be disturbed. This might be as simple as closing the door, or you might put something on display, as previously mentioned.

Make it clear that people can interrupt you for emergencies. You don't want your house to burn down, because your kid was worried about bothering you. In contrast, make it clear that unimportant things need to wait until you are on a break.

Tell Friends To Stay Away

While that might be a little drastic, you should ask your friends not to stop by and visit you during work hours. If someone wants to catch up, ask them to come visit during your lunch break, or make an appointment to see them after work. This is a difficult rule to enforce, because no one likes telling their friends to go away. Be polite about it, and just say that you are too busy to stop working, or else you would love to see them.

Keep Weekends And After Hours Sacred

It can be tempting to work a lot, especially when your office is down the hall from your living area. Don't give into that temptation. If you're single and live alone, sure, why not make as much money as you can. Just remember to stay sane by taking time off when you need a break.

For people who have families of their own — keep the weekends and after hours for *them*. Don't work late unless you absolutely must, and be sure that it does not happen too often. If you have the choice of putting in a little extra time on a Saturday, maybe just save it for the following work week. Never neglect your family so that you can work, especially when it's not a necessity.

Divide Up Your Work Day

For those who have household and family duties throughout the day, why not divide up your work day? Maybe you need to take your kids to school, so you can't start work until 10:00am. After that, you might have a solid block of time to work until they get off school at 3:00pm. Once they're fed and settled in, maybe your spouse will come home, or a babysitter arrives. Say it's about 5:00pm by the time you can go back to working. If you work until about 8:00pm, that's a full day's worth. In addition, you have managed to take care of your family duties, spend some quality time with your kids, and you still have the rest of the night to relax.

This is just an example of what a divided work day might be like. Even if you just need to do an extra hour or two at night, or in the early morning, that can help out greatly. Remember that you are the boss now, so you don't have to work from nine-till-five anymore!

Your Workspace

Find a Special Work Space

Hopefully you have an entire room that you can dedicate to your home office. It should preferably have a door that closes, and a lock might even be a nice idea, if you're *that* worried about distractions. Your work space does not need to be large, depending on what you do. For office work, you just need a desk or table and a comfortable chair. Your work space should have adequate lighting, with some natural light being preferable.

From this moment onward, this area is a *work zone*. Don't hang out in there and watch TV, or play games, or socialize. In fact, don't even think about putting a television set in your office. A radio or stereo is fine, if you like to listen to music as you work, although some computer speakers will probably be easier. Obtain any office equipment that you might need, like a filing cabinet or shelving system.

Some people don't have anywhere to work, so they are forced to accept a corner of their living room, or a space at the kitchen table. This is less than desirable, but you can certainly make it work. Just try to create a space that's as work friendly as possible, even if you have to clear out after work hours, so dinner can be made, or TV shows viewed.

Invest In Making Your Office Space Nice

You can work anywhere really, but there is a difference between productive work and stressful, trying-to-get-anything-done work. If you have the finances to set up a wonderful space, do so. It might cost a few thousand dollars, but that money is sure to come back to you in the future. Working in a nice, remodelled room is a lot better than sitting in your damp attic, in front of an old folding table, on a wobbly stool.

If you don't have much money to spend on your office, you can still make it pleasant to be in. You can print out some motivational posters, or images that you enjoy looking at. Stick them around where you work. Keep the temperature comfortable with a heater or air conditioner. Remember, you won't want to work if you're too uncomfortable. Provide adequate lighting so that you're not straining your eyes. Make sure that you have access to some fresh air, so that it doesn't get too stuffy. Find some beat up office furniture and paint it if you have to.

There are plenty of ways to make an office nicer. They might seem like small things, but a lot of little things adds up to make a nice office.

Consider Ergonomics

When you are choosing office furniture, think about your health. People might tell you that you're being too fussy, and you don't need any "fancy" equipment for work. If they are not office workers, how would they know what it's like to be at a desk for up to 12 hours a day? Even if they are, maybe they're just lucky enough that they haven't had any problems with repetitive strain injuries or back problems (yet).

You should have a fully ergonomic office chair, with adjustable backrest, and adjustable tilt and height. Sure, a $20 office chair will save you some money, and it might even be "good enough". More likely than not, it will break not very long after you buy it. In addition, a dodgy chair will cause problems for your spine and posture. If you need to save some money for a better chair, maybe you could use one from the kitchen for a while. Just be sure that it's a temporary thing, because office workers should definitely use proper chairs.

Your desk should also be at a suitable level for your height. That's why regular tables are often not ideal for computer work. If you are reaching up too high, or hunching down, and using a keyboard and mouse for long periods of time, it will cause you problems. If you want to use a regular table, buy a special keyboard tray that clamps on, with adjustable angle and height. That's a great way to turn any surface into a customizable, ergonomic workstation.

As for the height of your monitor, the top of it needs to be level with your eyes. That means that it will likely need to be on top of a raiser, or something else. There are plenty of sturdy items that you can use for this, so have a look around your home and shed. Otherwise, you can buy a purpose built monitor stand.

A foot rest is another great idea, and many people consider them a necessity. They're quite cheap, even for one that's adjustable.

Coffee Shops

Do you miss the hum and bustle of actual, living human beings? Many people like to take their laptops to coffee shops, so they can sit at a table and connect to the place's WiFi. It's best to find an establishment where the management is okay with this, however. Also understand that it is good etiquette to actually buy things from the cafe, and many places require that you do so. No one likes to be unable to find a place to eat their sandwich, because the seats are all occupied with freeloading workers.

Should You Rent Some Office Space?

Maybe you want some of the benefits of working from home, but you just can't get anything done there. There might come a time when it just makes sense to spend the extra money to rent some office space for yourself.

Here are the positive aspects of having a separate office space:

- All of the distractions that come with being around your family, and having access to everything in your home, can easily vanish.
- It will be simple to keep you work and person life separate. When you go to the office, everything is all about work. Once you get back home, work tasks stay behind.
- For people who are trying to maintain a professional image, having an office might be essential. In the world of business, working from home is still a relatively new thing. To impress clients and partners, it might make sense to keep your own office, even if you don't always use it.

Here are the negative aspects of having a separate office space:

- It's not as efficient on the whole, because you can't get little household things done during your breaks. Forget about putting on a load of laundry as you warm up your lunch, because you will not be at home.

- You will still need to commute to get to your office, instead of just walking down the hall.
- Your budget will need to be a lot larger, since you'll have to pay for rent or buy an office. And then there's the extra utility bills, phone line, and Internet connection to deal with.
- You can basically say goodbye to many of the benefits of working from home, even though you are still working for yourself, by yourself.

Staying Productive

It Only Takes Three Seconds To Get Distracted

Maybe you don't appreciate just how much little distractions can mess up your productivity.

A study that was released in 2013 showed that being distracted for just three seconds is enough to ruin your concentration. When asked to complete computer tasks, people's rate of error doubled after just a short interruption. Do you think that you can get work done while you're trying to do other things, like take care of a child, or cooking dinner? It is possible, but not likely.

Get Dressed Each Day

You might prefer to remain in your pajamas and slippers all day, and that is perfectly fine. But if you find that it's hard to click over into a work mindset, try dressing like you intend to actually go to work. Get up, have a shower, make yourself look presentable, and put on some comfortable business clothes. When they look the part, it's amazing how much more motivated some people feel.

Don't Sleep All Day

Getting plenty of sleep is important for everybody, but that doesn't mean sleeping for 15 hours a day. Your routine might allow that you get up at 10:00am, but that's probably a bad idea if you knock off at midday and go to bed early. People don't make money by lazing around in bed for half of each 24 hour period.

Wear Many Hats

Workplaces are typically made up of a range of different job positions. There are people who makes sales, others who answer the phones, and people who deal with finances and accounting. Those are just a few of the many different types of tasks that individuals take care of. When you work from home, guess what? You are going to need to take on more of those jobs, if not all of them. Unless you are outsourcing work to someone else, or remotely working for a larger company — learn to be happy wearing many different work hats.

Make A To-Do Lists And Stick To Them

With no boss to delegate tasks, it's your responsibility to make sure everything gets done. You should be keeping lists of the various tasks that need to get done, and when they are due. Each day, write out the things that you *need* to get done. These are your priorities for the day. Most people find that they can handle about three or so major tasks in a day. Anymore, and you might be overloading yourself, but everyone works at their own pace.

Next, you can add the lesser tasks that you would like to get done. Think of these as bonus tasks. If you can cross them off your list, great; if not, save them for tomorrow.

Be Careful With Your Time Management

Without a boss to guide you through the day, time management is a skill that you must become intimately familiar with. Buy books on the subject, read the blogs of successful business people, and ask a professional to help you organize your time if necessary. Whatever it takes to make sure that you are using your time efficiently — do it.

Okay, so some of the above ideas might be a little drastic for most people. You will need a system for scheduling your days, like a calendar or day planner. Next, you need to check it often, every day.

Eat Lunch At Your Desk

Instead of heading down to the local diner, or eating in front of the TV, take your lunch at your desk. This will make sure that you don't get *too* comfortable. Depriving yourself of just that tiny bit of home style comfort will also make it feel that you are really *at work*. This might seem like a silly idea to some people, but it can work.

Watch Your Snacking

Speaking of food, how many snacks have you eaten today? Being at home, with no one to judge you, and the pantry and fridge just in the next room — you are probably going to want some snacks. When you do break down and indulge yourself, try to keep it reasonable. A row of chocolate is a bit of a naughty treat in the middle of the day; an entire family sized block is more than just a treat, it's a possible habit. Be mindful of your snacking, and you will end up a lot happier and healthier.

The Social Media Trap

You're at home, you're on your computer working, and then suddenly — you think of something really funny that simply must be shared with your friends. And that is how is begins, when you fall into the "social media trap". As with any type of distraction, confine your *tweeting*, and *posting*, and *sharing*, and *following* to your off hours. Don't become a social media addict, when you are meant to be getting productive things done.

Unplug The Landline, Internet, Doorbell, Etc.

Maybe you need these things for work, or you probably just don't like to idea if disconnecting everything in your home, every time you want to get some work done. The point is, that you should limit outside distractions as much as possible. If the phone keeps ringing, and you don't need it for work, let an answering service deal with it until after office hours. Are you going to lose your mind if one more door knocking salesperson interrupts you in the middle of a brilliant thought? Put up a sign that tells people to leave you alone (in the most polite of way of course).

Keeping Yourself Motivated

Since there are so many new challenges waiting for people as they begin working at home, it is important to stay motivated. When you give yourself a task to do, make sure that it gets done. If there are deadlines coming up, there is no option but to meet them. There might not be anyone around to tell you off, except for maybe your clients, so you need to keep yourself in line.

Take Frequent Breaks

One of the best things about working from home, is that you can take a break at any given moment, usually. And you should as well! It is perfectly fine to get up every half our or so, and stretch out, maybe go to the bathroom, then return to work. As long as you only take a few minutes, this should be a good routine to get into. You will be surprised at how much more focused you feel after a quick break.

There Is Always Something Productive To Do

Sometimes you will finish a job in the middle of the day, and still be waiting for the go ahead to start your next project. That's wonderful, and it seems like a great chance to hit the couch, or go out for some shopping. Don't get tempted to quit working, even if you're not getting direct money for your hours.

There is always more to be done. Are your books balanced and your finances all in order? Is your office space starting to look like a garbage dump? Maybe you could be tracking down new leads, or sorting out a strategy for your next marketing campaign. During business hours, you should be working to further your career, no matter what.

FINANCES

Get An Accountant

You might be able to handle your own books, and deal with a budget. Even so, you should be in regular contact with a reliable, qualified accountant. They can tell you if you need to register for any special permits or tax statuses that are required in your area. It might be more efficient to pay someone else to do you, instead of spending hours on your own finances. It is well worth it in the long run.

Create A Financial Buffer

Working at home for yourself is like a roller coaster in many ways. Sometimes jobs will be coming in faster than you can manage to complete them. Other times, you can go days, or possibly a week or more, without a single job to do. Make sure that you create some savings for these dry spells. And that money should be earmarked as a buffer. Don't create a situation where you need to spend your vacation fund on groceries, because you didn't make a *separate* buffer fund.

Claim On Work Expenses

Since you are working from home, you might be able to claim a number of things when you file your tax return. Just like any other business, you might be exempt from paying tax for your office space, computer equipment, furniture, or stationery. The laws about this change from place to place, so it's best to look into it yourself. Make sure that you only claim what is legally allowed, otherwise

you might end up in some serious trouble
with the tax man.

Taking Care Of You

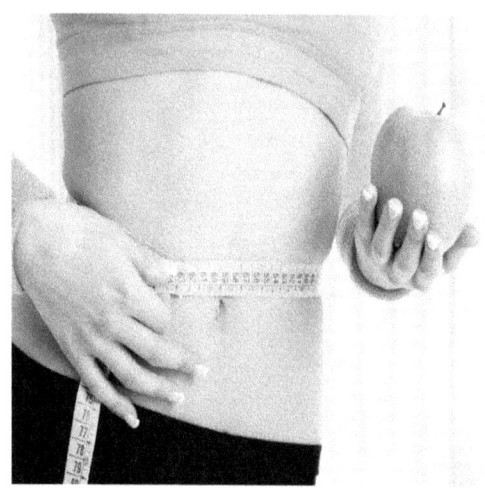

Stay Healthy

You are an important resource and, unless you want to wind up in line for a welfare check, it's essential to stay healthy. Don't burn the midnight oil and try to work all the time. Get enough sleep every night, and drink plenty of water. If junk food makes up the majority of your daily diet, introduce some fresh fruits and vegetables into your kitchen. No one is going to bail you out when you're too sick to work, because you've been living like a greasy teenager.

Make the Most of It

While you should certainly stay productive during work hours, it *is* alright to take advantage of your situation sometimes. Yes, "there is always something productive to do", but sometimes you need to reap the rewards of working at home. Does your kid have a school recital on during the day? It makes little sense to miss that, when you could easily catch that extra work time up later. Are you ill? Maybe sleeping in an extra hour or two would help you recover.

Stay on task and treat working from home just like any other job — to a degree. But remember that you *are* working from home, and you *can* take advantage of the perks occasionally.

Get Some Sun and Fresh Air

Even people who are cooped up in offices all day, get outside during their commute to and from work. If you take that away, it's easy to spend practically *all* of your time indoors. Soon, you might start to forget what sunlight actually feels like on your skin, or what fresh air smells like. You might not have to go outside today, but make an effort to stand in the sun's rays and take some deep breaths. It will not only clear your mind, but it will provide your body with essential vitamin D.

Join a Social Group

You will no longer be part of an employee social group, by default, any more. It just might save your sanity if you find a social group or club to become a member of. It doesn't really matter what you do there, so long as it provides you with the human contact that you have been longing for. Of course, some people crave isolation and quiet, so this tip isn't applicable to everyone.

Make Time for Yourself

This is something that is often overlooked, especially by people who have responsibilities to family. Always find a way to make some time for yourself. Ensure that you catch up with friends for some fun, and get out of the house once a week or so. Go on special date nights with your partner, so that they don't feel neglected. Buy yourself some nice work clothes, if that's something you enjoy. Take an afternoon off to see a movie, or go for a nice walk through the park.

No amount of money is going to make you happy if you forget to actually enjoy life. Treat yourself to the special, little things that make you feel good. Your productivity during work hours will improve, and you will find that you are able to earn more money.

It Will Get Better

Get this into your head right now: you are going to get stressed, overwhelmed, and feel like your time is stretched far too thin. When things seem bleak, and you feel too exhausted to get out of bed in the morning — just remember that things are going to get better. This is especially true for people who have only recently starting working from home. It's a big lifestyle adjustment, and it takes times to develop all the new habits that come along with that. Once you get into a good routine, the worry and tiredness is going to gradually melt away.

CONCLUSION

Working from home is a brave new world really. Many people are just realizing that they don't actually have to go to an office in order to bring home a pay check. With the rise in computer related jobs, as well as self-employment opportunities, there is no reason why you can't work from home. In this way, it's possible to "have your cake and eat it too"!

Have you decided to get the best of both worlds, and carefully merge your home life with your job? Things might be difficult at first, and there are sure to be some upset family members in your house. Just keep at it, and find the routine that works best for *you*. After all, you are in charge of your own days now, and there's no reason why you can't work from home and stay sane!